I'm Thinking of an Ocean State

Bela Davis

Abdo Kids Junior
is an Imprint of Abdo Kids
abdobooks.com

Abdo
I'M THINKING OF A STATE
Kids

abdobooks.com

Published by Abdo Kids, a division of ABDO, P.O. Box 398166, Minneapolis, Minnesota 55439.

Printed in the United States of America, North Mankato, Minnesota.

102025

012026

THIS BOOK CONTAINS RECYCLED MATERIALS

Photo Credits: Alamy, Getty Images, Shutterstock

Production Contributors: Teddy Borth, Jennie Forsberg, Grace Hansen

Design Contributors: Candice Keimig, Pakou Moua

Library of Congress Control Number: 2025936502

Publisher's Cataloging-in-Publication Data

Names: Davis, Bela, author.

Title: I'm thinking of an ocean state / by Bela Davis

Description: Minneapolis, Minnesota : Abdo Kids, 2026 | Series: I'm thinking of a state | Includes online resources and index.

Identifiers: ISBN 9798384907404 (lib. bdg.) | ISBN 9798384908104 (ebook) | ISBN 9798384908456 (Read-to-Me ebook)

Subjects: LCSH: Coastal zones--Juvenile literature. | American states (United States)--Juvenile literature. | Geography--Juvenile literature. | Physical geography--United States--Juvenile literature.

Classification: DDC 917--dc23

Table of Contents

Guess the State!

I'm thinking of an ocean state! It is a state that touches the Atlantic or Pacific oceans.

N
W
E
S
Alaska
Pacific Ocean
New Hampshire
Massachusetts
Maine
New York
Rhode Island
Connecticut
New Jersey
Delaware
Maryland
Virginia
North Carolina
South Carolina
Georgia
Florida
Atlantic Ocean
Pacific Ocean
Hawaii

Can you guess the state?

The state flower is the yellow jessamine.

State Clues

- **Flower:** Yellow jessamine

7

The state bird is a type of wren.

State Clues

- **Flower:** Yellow jessamine
- **Bird:** Wren

Green **anoles** can be found in this state. They can change their color!

State Clues

- **Flower:** Yellow jessamine
- **Bird:** Wren
- **Animal:** Green anole

People surf in this state!

State Clues

- **Flower:** Yellow jessamine
- **Bird:** Wren
- **Animal:** Green anole
- **Activity:** Surfing

People take boat trips in this state. They might see dolphins!

State Clues

- **Flower:** Yellow jessamine
- **Bird:** Wren
- **Animal:** Green anole
- **Activity:** Surfing
- **Visit:** Dolphins

SEA WOLF II
SEA WOLF II

People explore Congaree National Park in this state.

State Clues

• Flower:	Yellow jessamine
• Bird:	Wren
• Animal:	Green anole
• Activity:	Surfing
• Visit:	Dolphins
• Explore:	Congaree

The state's capital is Columbia.

State Clues

- **Flower:** Yellow jessamine
- **Bird:** Wren
- **Animal:** Green anole
- **Activity:** Surfing
- **Visit:** Dolphins
- **Explore:** Congaree
- **Capital:** Columbia

Now you have all the clues! Can you guess what state I'm thinking of?

State Clues

• Flower:	Yellow jessamine
• Bird:	Wren
• Animal:	Green anole
• Activity:	Surfing
• Visit:	Dolphins
• Explore:	Congaree
• Capital:	Columbia

NC
HI
FL
SC

I'm Thinking of...

South Carolina!

Glossary

anole

any of the various mainly tropical lizards that can change color. Males usually have a brightly colored flap of skin on the throat.

national park

a special area of land that is set aside by the United States government to protect it.

Index